Savvy
Single Crochet™

General Information

Many of the products used in this pattern book can be purchased from local craft, fabric and variety stores, or from the Annie's Attic Needlecraft Catalog (see Customer Service information on page 16).

Welcome to a fun and easy way to crochet!!

Savvy Single Crochet is based on the technique American single crochet *(known internationally as double crochet)*. By changing the placement of your stitches and using a larger size hook than you would normally with the yarn you are using, the fabric gives the look of knit, with a softer drape and feel.

Another feature of using this technique is that you use less yarn than you would in normal crochet. The larger hook size and the "taller" stitches allow your item to be completed more quickly, too!

This book includes instructions on how to form the 6 basic stitches. Once you have learned the stitches, I have several simple patterns to help you get started.

Try it with fashion yarns, crochet thread, even twine or rope to create new textures and fabrics that will delight everyone!

Karen Whooly

Basic Stitch Instructions

The single crochet stitch is probably the most common stitch used in crochet. Whether you are new to crochet, or have been crocheting for more years than you can count, you will find that this technique is easy to learn and fun to do.

TERMINOLOGY AND ABBREVIATIONS

As with learning any crochet technique, there are always new terms and abbreviations to learn. That is no different with *Savvy Single Crochet*.

The table below includes all the terms and abbreviations that you will be using in this book.

STITCH OR TERM	ABBREVIATION
Back loops only	bk lps only
Back-knit single stitch	bk-kss
Chain	ch
Double back-knit single stitch	db-kss
Double knit single stitch	d-kss
End loops	end lps
Knitted single stitch	kss
Rear loop of chain	rlp-ch
Rear loop of stitch	rlp-st
Single crochet	sc
Skip	sk
Stitch	st
Savvy Single Crochet	SSC
Twisted single stitch	tss
V-knit single stitch	V-kss
Front loops only	ft lps only

SIMPLE DEFINITIONS
WORKING IN THE STARTING CHAIN

In traditional crochet, the starting row is worked with the front of the chain facing forward *(see Photo A)*. To create the base for Savvy Single Crochet, the chain is turned backwards.

A **Front of Chain**

You will notice *(see Photo B)* that there are loops/nubs coming through the center which join the chains together. These are **rear loop chains** *(rlp-ch)* or **back bar of chain** *(see Fig. 1)*.

B **Back of Chain**

Fig. 1
Back Bar of Chain

WORKING IN REAR LOOP OF STITCH (RLP-ST) AND WORKING IN FRONT & BACK LOOPS (BK LPS, FT LPS)

In traditional crochet, stitches are worked on top of each other through the front and back loops of the stitches of the previous row/round *(see Photo C)*.

Now you will work your single crochets in the loop on the back side of the stitch just underneath the back loop of the stitch *(see Photo D)*. This is the **rear loop** stitch *(rlp-st)* or **back bar of single crochet** *(see Fig. 2)*.

Fig. 2
Back Bar of Single Crochet

WORKING IN THE END LOOPS

Because you are always skipping the first stitch of the row *(when working in rows)*, you will have to add a stitch to the end of each row. The skipped stitch of the previous row will create 2 visible loops called the end loops *(end lps, see Photo E and F)*.

6 BASIC STITCHES

Let's get started with learning the basic stitches. For any of these stitches, you can make a starting chain for whatever length you wish. However, for our sample swatches, use the suggested chain indicated in the stitch.

KNITTED SINGLE STITCH

KNITTED SINGLE STITCH (KSS)

Row 1: Ch 20, sc in the rear lp of each ch across, turn. *(20 sc)*

Row 2: Ch 1, sc in rear lp of 2nd sc from hook and in each sc across, sc in end lps, turn.

Rep row 2 for pattern.

**Knitted Single Stitch Ripple Afghan
Page 12**

DOUBLE-KNIT SINGLE STITCH

DOUBLE-KNIT SINGLE STITCH (D-KSS)

Row 1: Ch 20, sc in the rear lp of each ch across, turn. *(20 sc)*

Row 2: Ch 1, sc in rear lp and front lp of 2nd st and in each st across, sc in end lps, turn.

Rep row 2 for pattern.

**Double-Knit Single Stitch Dishcloth
Page 11**

V-KNIT SINGLE STITCH

TWISTED SINGLE STITCH

V-KNIT SINGLE STITCH (V-KSS)

Row 1: Ch 20, sc in the rear lp of each ch across, turn. *(20 sc)*

Row 2: Ch 1, sc in rear lp and both lps of 2nd sc and in each sc across, sc in end lp, turn.

Rep row 2 for pattern.

TWISTED SINGLE STITCH (TSS)

Row 1: Ch 20, sc in the rear lp of each ch across, turn. *(20 sc)*

Row 2: Ch 1, sc from top to bottom in rear lp of 2nd sc and in each sc across, sc in end lps, turn.

Rep row 2 for pattern.

**V-Knit Single Stitch Baby Blanket
Page 7**

**Twisted Single Stitch Runner
Page 10**

BACK-KNIT SINGLE STITCH

DOUBLE BACK-KNIT SINGLE STITCH

BACK-KNIT SINGLE STITCH (BK-KSS)

Note: For this st, each row is worked on the same side. Also, you will not sk the first st of the previous row and you will not work in the end lps.

Also, note that this st is actually better suited to be worked in the rnd. In that case, you would not need to fasten off at the end of every rnd, leaving lp. A simple spiral is all that is needed.

Row 1: Ch 20, sc in the rear lp of each ch across, cut yarn, **do not fasten off**, leave last lp at end of row. *(20 sc)*

Row 2: With RS facing, sc in rear lp of first st by inserting hook downward into lp, sc in this manner across to last st, place lp from last row on hook, yo, pull through both lps on hook, cut yarn, **do not fasten off**, leave last lp at end of row.

Rep row 2 for pattern.

DOUBLE BACK-KNIT SINGLE STITCH (DB-KSS)

Note: For this st, each row is worked on the same side. Also, you will not sk the first st of the previous row, and you will not work in the end lps.

Also, note that this st is actually better suited to be worked in the rnd. In that case, you would not need to fasten off at the end of every rnd, leaving lp. A simple spiral is all that is needed.

Row 1: Ch 20, sc in the rear lp of each ch across, cut yarn, **do not fasten off**, leave last lp at end of row. *(20 sc)*

Row 2: With RS facing, join with sc in back lp and rear lp in first st by inserting hook downward into back lp and rear lp, sc in same manner in each st across to last st, place lp from last row on hook, yo, pull through both lps on hook, cut yarn, **do not fasten off**, leave last lp at end of row.

Rep row 2 for pattern.

**Back-Knit Single Stitch Rug
Page 8**

**Double Back-Knit Single Stitch
Round Dishcloth Page 13**

V-Knit Single Stitch
Baby Blanket

SKILL LEVEL

EASY

FINISHED SIZE
33 inches wide x 39½ inches long

MATERIALS
- Medium (worsted) weight yarn
  (2 oz/95 yds/57g per ball):
    22 oz/1,045 yds/624g white
- Size K/10½/6.5mm crochet hook
  or size needed to obtain gauge

GAUGE
10 pattern sts = 4 inches; 13 pattern rows =
4 inches

PATTERN NOTE
Join with slip stitch as indicated unless
  otherwise stated.

PATTERN
V-Knit Single Stitch (V-kss): See V-knit single
  stitch in Basic Stitch Instructions on page 5.

INSTRUCTIONS
AFGHAN
Row 1: Ch 76, sc in **rlp-ch** (*see Basic Stitch
Instructions on page 2*) in 2nd ch from hook
and in each ch across, turn. (*75 sc*)

Rows 2–119: Ch 1, **V-kss** (*see Pattern*) in 2nd st
and in each st across, **end lps** (*see Basic Stitch
Instructions on page 2*), turn.

EDGING
Rnd 1: Now working in rnds and in ends of rows,
ch 1, 3 sc in first st (*corner*), sc in each st across
with 3 sc in last st (*corner*), evenly sp 115 sc in
ends of rows across, working in starting ch on
opposite side of row 1, 3 sc in first ch (*corner*),
sc in each ch across with 3 sc in last ch (*corner*),
evenly sp 115 sc in ends of rows across, **join**
(*see Pattern Note*) in beg sc. (*388 sc*)

Rnd 2: Working in **back lps** (*see Basic Stitch
Instructions on page 2*), ch 1, sc in each st
around with 3 sc in each center corner st, join
in beg sc. (*396 sc*)

Rnd 3: Sl st in each of next 2 sts, ch 1, sc in same
st, *sk next 2 sts, 5 dc in next st**, sk next 2 sts,
sc in next st, rep from * around, ending last rep
at **, sk last st, join in beg sc. Fasten off. ∎

Back-Knit Single Stitch RUG

SKILL LEVEL

EASY

FINISHED SIZE
19 inches wide x 32 inches long

MATERIALS
- Caron Craft and Rug yarn bulky (chunky) weight yarn (1½ oz/49 yds/ 43g per ball):
    6 balls #0008 spice
- Size N/15/10mm crochet hook or size needed to obtain gauge
- Stitch marker

GAUGE
9 pattern sts = 4 inches

PATTERN NOTES
Work in continuous rounds, do not turn or join unless otherwise stated.

Mark first stitch of round.

Work in rear loop of each stitch unless otherwise stated.

PATTERN
Back-knit single stitch (b-kss): See back-knit single stitch in Basic Stitch Instructions on page 6.

INSTRUCTIONS
RUG
Rnd 1: Ch 41, 3 sc in **rlp-ch** *(see Basic Stitch Instructions on page 2)* in 2nd ch from hook, sc in each of next 38 chs, 3 sc in last ch, working on opposite side of ch, sc in each ch across, **do not join** *(see Pattern Notes)*. *(82 sc)*

Rnd 2: Working in **rlp-st** *(see Basic Stitch Instructions on page 2 and Pattern Notes)*, 2 **b-kss** *(see Pattern)* in each of next 3 sts, b-kss in each of next 38 sts, 2 b-kss in each of next 3 sts, b-kss in each st around. *(88 b-kss)*

Rnd 3: B-kss in each st around.

Rnd 4: *[B-kss in next st, 2 b-kss in next st] 3 times, b-kss in each of next 38 sts, rep from * once. *(94 b-kss)*

Rnd 5: *[B-kss in each of next 2 sts, 2 b-kss in next st] 3 times, b-kss in each of next 38 sts, rep from * once. *(100 b-kss)*

Rnd 6: B-kss in each st around.

Rnd 7: *[B-kss in each of next 3 sts, 2 b-kss in next st] 3 times, b-kss in each of next 38 sts, rep from * once. *(106 b-kss)*

Rnd 8: *[2 b-kss in next st, b-kss in each of next 4 sts] 3 times, b-kss in each of next 38 sts, rep from * once. *(112 b-kss)*

Rnd 9: B-kss in each st around.

Rnd 10: *[B-kss in each of next 5 sts, 2 b-kss in next st] 3 times, b-kss in each of next 38 sts, rep from * once. *(118 b-kss)*

Rnd 11: *[2 b-kss in next st, b-kss in each of next 6 sts] 3 times, b-kss in each of next 38 sts, rep from * once. *(124 b-kss)*

Rnd 12: B-kss in each st around.

Rnd 13: *[B-kss in each of next 7 sts, 2 b-kss in next st] 3 times, b-kss in each of next 38 sts, rep from * once. *(130 b-kss)*

Rnd 14: *[2 b-kss in next st, b-kss in each of next 8 sts] 3 times, b-kss in each of next 38 sts, rep from * once. *(136 b-kss)*

Rnd 15: B-kss in each st around.

Rnd 16: *[B-kss in each of next 9 sts, 2 b-kss in next st] 3 times, b-kss in each of next 38 sts, rep from * once. *(142 b-kss)*

Rnd 17: *[2 b-kss in next st, b-kss in each of next 10 sts] 3 times, b-kss in each of next 38 sts, rep from * once. *(148 b-kss)*

Rnd 18: B-kss in each st around.

Rnd 19: *[B-kss in each of next 11 sts, 2 b-kss in next st] 3 times, b-kss in each of next 38 sts, rep from * once. *(154 b-kss)*

Rnd 20: *[2 b-kss in next st, b-kss in each of next 12 sts] 3 times, b-kss in each of next 38 sts, rep from * once. *(160 b-kss)*

Rnd 21: B-kss in each st around.

Rnd 22: Sl st in rear lp of each st around. Fasten off.

Block to finished size if needed. ∎

Twisted Single Stitch Runner

SKILL LEVEL

EASY

FINISHED SIZE
18 inches wide x 40 inches long

MATERIALS
- Aunt Lydia's Fashion Crochet size 3 crochet cotton (150 yds per ball):
    5 balls #175 warm blue
    1 ball #201p white/pearl
- Size G/6/4mm crochet hook or size needed to obtain gauge
- Stitch marker

GAUGE
20 pattern sts = 4 inches; 16 pattern rows = 4 inches

PATTERN NOTES
Work in continuous rounds, do not turn or join unless otherwise stated.

Mark first stitch of round.

PATTERN
Twisted single stitch (tss): See Twisted Single Stitch in Basic Stitch Instructions on page 5.

INSTRUCTIONS
RUNNER
Row 1: With blue, ch 191, sc in **rlp-ch** *(see Basic Stitch Instructions on page 2)* in 2nd ch from hook and in each ch across, turn. *(190 sc)*

Rows 2–64: Ch 1, **tss** *(see Pattern)* across, sc in **end lps** *(see Basic Stitch Instructions on page 2)*, turn. At end of last row, fasten off.

EDGING
Rnd 1: With RS facing, join white with sc in first st, 2 sc in same st *(corner)*, sc in each st across to last st, 3 sc in last st *(corner)*, working in ends of rows, evenly sp 62 sc across, working in starting ch on opposite side of row 1, 3 sc in first ch *(corner)*, sc in each ch across with 3 sc in last ch *(corner)*, evenly sp 62 sc in ends of rows across, **do not join** *(see Pattern Notes)*. *(512 sc)*

Rnds 2–5: Sc in each st around with 3 sc in each center corner st. At end of last rnd, join with sl st in beg sc. *(544 sc at end of last rnd)*

Rnd 6: Ch 1, sc in first st, [ch 3, sl st in 3rd ch from hook, sc in each of next 3 sts] around, join with sl st in beg sc. Fasten off. ∎

Double-Knit Single Stitch
Dishcloth

SKILL LEVEL

EASY

FINISHED SIZE
8 x 10 inches

MATERIALS
- Lily Sugar'n Cream medium (worsted) weight cotton yarn (2½ oz/ 120 yds/71g per ball):
  1 ball #00083 cornflower blue
- Size K/10½/6.5mm crochet hook or size needed to obtain gauge

GAUGE
12 pattern sts = 4 inches

PATTERN
Double-Knit Single Stitch (d-kss): See double-knit single stitch in Basic Stitch Instructions on page 4.

INSTRUCTIONS
DISHCLOTH
Row 1: Ch 25, sc in **rlp-ch** *(see Basic Stitch Instructions on page 2)* in 2nd ch from hook and in each ch across, turn. *(24 sc)*

Row 2: Ch 1, **d-kss** *(see Pattern)* in 2nd st and in each st across, **end lps** *(see Basic Stitch Instructions on page 2)*, turn.

Rows 3–30: Rep row 2. At end of last row, **do not turn**.

EDGING
Working in ends of rows, sts and starting ch on opposite side of row 1 and from left to right, evenly sp **reverse sc** *(see Fig. 1)* around, join in beg reverse sc. Fasten off. ∎

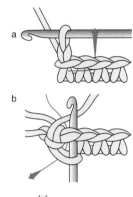

Fig. 1
Reverse Single Crochet

Knitted Single Stitch
Ripple Afghan

SKILL LEVEL

EASY

FINISHED SIZE
50 x 65 inches

MATERIALS

- Caron Simply Soft Tweed bulky (chunky) weight yarn (3 oz/150 yds/ 85g per skein):
  18 skeins #0007 autumn red
- Size K/10½/6.5mm crochet hook or size needed to obtain gauge

GAUGE
1 chevron = 5 inches

PATTERN
Knit Single Stitch (kss): See knit single stitch in Basic Stitch Instructions on page 4.

INSTRUCTIONS
AFGHAN
Row 1: Ch 255, sc in **rlp-ch** *(see Basic Stitch Instructions on page 2)*, sc in 2nd ch from hook and in next ch, sk next ch, *sc in each of next 11 chs, 3 sc in next ch, sc in each of next 11 chs**, sk next 2 chs rep from * across, ending last rep at **, sk next ch, sc in each of last 2 chs, turn. *(10 chevrons)*

Row 2: Ch 1, sc in each of first 2 sts, sk next st, ***kss** *(see Pattern)* in each of next 11 sts, 3 kss in next st, kss in each of next 11 sts**, sk next 2 sts, rep from * across, ending last rep at **, sk next st, sc in both lps in each of last 2 sts, turn.

Next rows: Rep row 2 until piece measures 65 inches long. At end of last row, fasten off. ■

Double Back-Knit Single Stitch
Round Dishcloth

SKILL LEVEL

EASY

FINISHED SIZE
9¼ inches in diameter

MATERIALS
- Bernat Handicrafter Cotton Stripes medium (worsted) weight cotton yarn (1½ oz/68 yds/43g per ball):
    1 ball #21143 country stripes
- Size K/10½/6.5mm crochet hook or size needed to obtain gauge
- Stitch marker

GAUGE
7 pattern rnds = 4 inches in diameter

PATTERN NOTES
Work in continuous rounds, do not turn or join unless otherwise stated.

Mark first stitch of round.

PATTERN
Double Back-Knit Single Stitch (db-kss): See double back-knit single stitch in Basic Stitch Instructions on page 6.

INSTRUCTIONS
DISHCLOTH
Rnd 1: Ch 2, 6 sc in **rlp-ch** *(see Basic Stitch Instructions on page 2)* of 2nd ch from hook, **do not join** *(see Pattern Notes)*. *(6 sc)*

Rnd 2: 2 **db-kss** *(see Pattern)* in each st around. *(12 db-kss)*

Rnd 3: [Db-kss in next st, 2 db-kss in next st] around. *(18 db-kss)*

Rnd 4: [Db-kss in each of next 2 sts, 2 db-kss in next st] around. *(24 db-kss)*

Rnd 5: [Db-kss in each of next 3 sts, 2 db-kss in next st] around. *(30 db-kss)*

Rnd 6: [Db-kss in each of next 4 sts, 2 db-kss in next st] around. *(36 db-kss)*

Rnd 7: [Db-kss in each of next 5 sts, 2 db-kss in next st] around. *(42 db-kss)*

Rnd 8: [Db-kss in each of next 6 sts, 2 db-kss in next st] around. *(48 db-kss)*

Rnd 9: [Db-kss in each of next 7 sts, 2 db-kss in next st] around. *(54 db-kss)*

Rnd 10: [Db-kss in each of next 8 sts, 2 db-kss in next st] around. *(60 db-kss)*

Rnd 11: [Db-kss in each of next 9 sts, 2 db-kss in next st] around. *(66 db-kss)*

Rnd 12: [Db-kss in each of next 10 sts, 2 db-kss in next st] around. *(72 db-kss)*

Rnd 13: [Db-kss in each of next 11 sts, 2 db-kss in next st] around. *(78 db-kss)*

Rnd 14: [Db-kss in each of next 12 sts, 2 db-kss in next st] around. *(84 db-kss)*

EDGING
[Ch 3, sl st in 3rd ch from hook, db-kss in each of next 3 sts] around, join with sl st in beg db-kss. Fasten off. ■

Stitch Guide

For more complete information, visit **FreePatterns.com**

ABBREVIATIONS

beg	begin/begins/beginning
bpdc	back post double crochet
bpsc	back post single crochet
bptr	back post treble crochet
CC	contrasting color
ch(s)	chain(s)
ch-	refers to chain or space previously made (i.e. ch-1 space)
ch sp(s)	chain space(s)
cl(s)	cluster(s)
cm	centimeter(s)
dc	double crochet (singular/plural)
dc dec	double crochet 2 or more stitches together, as indicated
dec	decrease/decreases/decreasing
dtr	double treble crochet
ext	extended
fpdc	front post double crochet
fpsc	front post single crochet
fptr	front post treble crochet
g	gram(s)
hdc	half double crochet
hdc dec	half double crochet 2 or more stitches together, as indicated
inc	increase/increases/increasing
lp(s)	loop(s)
MC	main color
mm	millimeter(s)
oz	ounce(s)
pc	popcorn(s)
rem	remain/remains/remaining
rep(s)	repeat(s)
rnd(s)	round(s)
RS	right side
sc	single crochet (singular/plural)
sc dec	single crochet 2 or more stitches together, as indicated
sk	skip/skipped/skipping
sl st(s)	slip stitch(es)
sp(s)	space(s)/spaced
st(s)	stitch(es)
tog	together
tr	treble crochet
trtr	triple treble
WS	wrong side
yd(s)	yard(s)
yo	yarn over

Chain—ch: Yo, pull through lp on hook.

Slip stitch—sl st: Insert hook in st, pull through both lps on hook.

Single crochet—sc: Insert hook in st, yo, pull through st, yo, pull through both lps on hook.

Front post stitch—fp: Back post stitch—bp: When working post st, insert hook from right to left around post st on previous row.

Back   Front

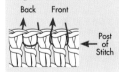

← Post of Stitch

Front loop—front lp Back loop—back lp

Front Loop   Back Loop

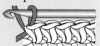

Half double crochet—hdc: Yo, insert hook in st, yo, pull through st, yo, pull through all 3 lps on hook.

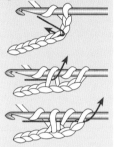

Double crochet—dc: Yo, insert hook in st, yo, pull through st, [yo, pull through 2 lps] twice.

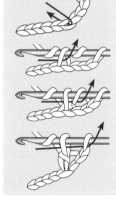

Change colors: Drop first color; with 2nd color, pull through last 2 lps of st.

Treble crochet—tr: Yo twice, insert hook in st, yo, pull through st, [yo, pull through 2 lps] 3 times.

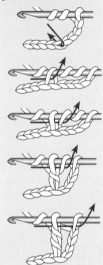

Double treble crochet—dtr: Yo 3 times, insert hook in st, yo, pull through st, [yo, pull through 2 lps] 4 times.

Single crochet decrease (sc dec): (Insert hook, yo, draw lp through) in each of the sts indicated, yo, draw through all lps on hook.

Example of 2-sc dec

Half double crochet decrease (hdc dec): (Yo, insert hook, yo, draw lp through) in each of the sts indicated, yo, draw through all lps on hook.

Example of 2-hdc dec

Double crochet decrease (dc dec): (Yo, insert hook, yo, draw loop through, draw through 2 lps on hook) in each of the sts indicated, yo, draw through all lps on hook.

Example of 2-dc dec

Example of 2-tr dec

Treble crochet decrease (tr dec): Holding back last lp of each st, tr in each of the sts indicated, yo, pull through all lps on hook.

US		UK
sl st (slip stitch)	=	sc (single crochet)
sc (single crochet)	=	dc (double crochet)
hdc (half double crochet)	=	htr (half treble crochet)
dc (double crochet)	=	tr (treble crochet)
tr (treble crochet)	=	dtr (double treble crochet)
dtr (double treble crochet)	=	ttr (triple treble crochet)
skip	=	miss

TOLL-FREE ORDER LINE or to request a free catalog (800) LV-ANNIE (800) 582-6643
Customer Service (800) AT-ANNIE (800) 282-6643, **Fax** (800) 882-6643
Visit anniesattic.com

We have made every effort to ensure the accuracy and completeness of these instructions.
We cannot, however, be responsible for human error, typographical mistakes or variations in individual work.

ISBN: 978-1-59635-228-5

Printed in USA

1 2 3 4 5 6 7 8 9